Concertino

for Clarinet and String Orchestra

selected and arranged
from Sonatas of

Giuseppe Tartini

by Gordon Jacob

Clarinet and Piano

BOOSEY & HAWKES

AN IMAGEM COMPANY

DISTRIBUTED BY

HAL•LEONARD®
CORPORATION
7777 W. BLUEMOUND RD. P.O. BOX 13819 MILWAUKEE, WI 53213

The clarinet, compared with the flute, oboe and bassoon, is a modern instrument and therefore little or no music written before the time of Mozart exists for it. This is a misfortune, for it means that a golden age of music, which included Handel and Bach and a host of lesser but admirable composers, has hitherto been a closed book to clarinettists.

This little work is a free arrangement of movements taken from two of Tartini's sonatas for violin.

G.J.

IMPORTANT NOTICE
The unauthorised copying
of the whole or any part of
this publication is illegal

CONCERTINO

GIUSEPPE TARTINI (1692-1770)
Arranged by GORDON JACOB

I

© Copyright 1945 by Hawkes & Son (London) Ltd.; Renewed 1973.
Copyright for all countries. All rights reserved.

B.W.I.131   Printed in U.S.A.

4

II

Allegro molto

8

B.& H. 9028

CONCERTINO

IMPORTANT NOTICE
The unauthorised copying of the whole or any part of this publication is illegal

Clarinet in B♭

GIUSEPPE TARTINI (1692-1770)
Arranged by GORDON JACOB

I

II

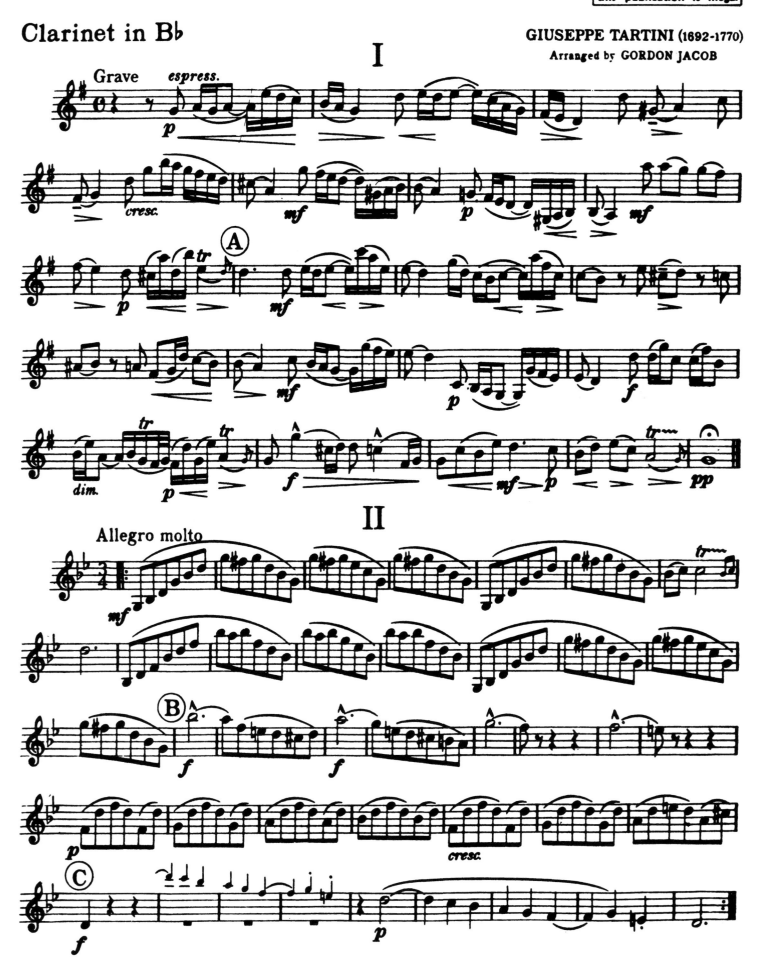

Copyright 1945 in U.S.A. by Hawkes & Sons (London) Ltd.; Renewed 1973
Copyright for all countries. All rights reserved.

WCB-7

Printed in U.S.A.

Clarinet in B♭

III

Adagio

IV

Allegro risoluto

Clarinet in B♭

III

Adagio

IV

Allegro risoluto